S0-DGL-842

Quick Start Internet Marketing Toolkit

Jeff Paul

© 2007 Shortcuts to Internet Millions, LLC - All Rights Reserved Worldwide

www.BigLeaguePlayersClub.com

ALL RIGHTS RESERVED. No part of this book may be reproduced or transmitted for resale or use by any party other than the individual purchaser who is the sole authorized user of this information. Purchaser is authorized to use any of the information in this publication for his or her own use only. All other reproduction or transmission, or any form or by any means, electronic or mechanical, including photocopying, recording or by any informational storage or retrieval system, is prohibited without express written permission from the publisher.

LEGAL NOTICES: While all attempts have been made to provide effective, verifiable information in this Book, neither the Author nor Publisher assumes any responsibility for errors, inaccuracies, or omissions. Any slights of people or organizations are unintentional. If advice concerning tax, legal, compliance, or related matters is needed, the services of a qualified professional should be sought. This Book is not a source of legal, regulatory compliance, or accounting information, and it should not be regarded as such. This publication is designed to provide accurate and authoritative information in regard to the subject matter covered. It is sold with the understanding that the publisher is not engaged in rendering legal, accounting or other professional service. If legal advice or other expert assistance is required, the services of a competent professional person should be sought. Due to the nature of direct response marketing and varying rules regulating business activities in many fields, some practices proposed in this Book may be deemed unlawful in certain circumstances and locations. Since federal and local laws differ widely, as do codes of conduct for members of professional organizations and agencies, Licensee must accept full responsibility for determining the legality and/or ethical character of any and all business transactions and/or practices adopted and enacted in his or her particular field and geographic location, whether or not those transactions and/or practices are suggested, either directly or indirectly, in this Book. As with any business advice, the reader is strongly encouraged to seek professional counsel before taking action. NOTE: No guarantees of income or profits are intended by this book. Many variables affect each individual's results. Your results will vary from the examples given. Jeff Paul, Jeff Paul, LLC and Shortcuts to Internet Millions, LLC cannot and will not promise your personal success and has no control over what you may do or not do with this program, and therefore cannot accept the responsibility for your results. You are the only one who can initiate the action, in order to reap your own rewards! Any and all references to persons or businesses, whether living or dead, existing or defunct, are purely coincidental.

Published by: Shortcuts to Internet Millions, LLC
PRINTED IN THE UNITED STATES OF AMERICA DISTRIBUTED WORLDWIDE.

© 2007 Shortcuts to Internet Millions, LLC

Table of Contents

© 2007 Shortcuts to Internet Millions, LLC - All Rights Reserved Worldwide
www.BigLeaguePlayersClub.com

This page intentionally left blank

© 2007 Shortcuts to Internet Millions, LLC - All Rights Reserved Worldwide

www.BigLeaguePlayersClub.com

Introduction

As I sit here writing this introduction at home, sitting at my kitchen table, in my underwear, I still can't believe how much the Internet has opened up new marketing avenues and increased the marketing power of our promotions.

At no other time have I been able to sit at my desktop and create products and services, and emails and conduct a business even easier at home than I could before. With the advent of the Internet, I can communicate with my vendors, my clients, my customers' clients and patients, and anyone else.

Research has shown there are a growing number of people that are quitting the rat race and they are escaping to jobs that they actually either work from home at or they are starting their own businesses and working from home.

In the early days of the Internet, the speed was slow, the tools were lacking and the information was very archaic. While today, the tools are powerful, the speed is getting faster and faster with the advent of DSL and cable modems, and the content is oftentimes cutting edge.

But there is so much information on the Internet that you can get lost. It is the information superhighway and oftentimes without a map, you will find yourself driving aimlessly from location to location.

So, in Quick Start Toolkit we're going to help you:

- Achieve quick and easier profits
- Reduce your investment of time and money
- Avoid major mistakes
- Avoid major headaches and hassles
- We're going to help you automate and streamlines your Internet business where possible to help you get more leverage out of your Internet sites
- We're going to help you clear up the sheer confusion of how to conduct business on the Internet
- We're going to point out where possible the con artists and the rip-off schemes and we're going to help you avoid time wasters

One of the best things about Quick Start Toolkit is you have a ready-made update mechanism in place.

We're going to be teaching you, based on the experience and knowledge of many Internet marketers that have been out on the front lines for almost the last 10 years, and we've worked long and hard to make sure this material is current and relevant and that it's a good resource and any additional things we come up with or items that need to be changed.

© 2007 Shortcuts to Internet Millions, LLC - All Rights Reserved Worldwide

www.BigLeaguePlayersClub.com

For updates and all the latest changes that have come about since this book went to print, go to: http://www.BigLeaguePlayersClub.com. For your free gift, simply click the "Register" button.

Chapter 1
Do People Really Make Money On The Internet?

That's the big question. And of course, the next question is, if people do make money on the Internet, how are they doing it and how can I do the same thing to make money in my own Internet business?

To show you how some people have built profitable businesses on-line and to show you that you can to, I am going to talk about some examples of people that have done this.

And then throughout the rest of Quick Start Toolkit, we'll go into details on what some of these people have done, some of the principles they've used, and some of the strategies they've used and you can too to build your profitable Internet business. So let's get started with the first example.

One client has constantly been on the front lines and out there doing it. He has been looking at Internet sites, finding ways to make them better, he actually goes out to ebay.com to the area where people sell websites and he looks for websites that are under utilized, in other words, they seem to have some traffic, they seem to have some sales, but their owners just really don't know what they're doing or don't value the site.

He then goes out there and makes an offer on those Internet sites. He takes those sites from the owners in exchange for his bid price, and then he instantly goes out and joint ventures with other Internet sites all over the place that market to the same types of customers, so he instantly boosts the traffic to that site which, of course, gets sales.

He then captures email addresses by giving away something very valuable, and then he uses what he calls linking strategies to create a web of resources of other like minded Internet sites so that they will also link back to him. So, he instantly creates a bond and creates a network of sites, and then he builds up the traffic and sales, and he goes out and sells it for 5, 10, 15 times what he bought it for.

Another client has built his subscriber list using all the techniques that we mention in this program, from zero subscribers to 60,000 subscribers in one year.

He goes out and he finds unique books, rare books, he reads them and distills the information down into book summaries. He then sends those book summaries out in his ezine to his subscriber list of 60,000 people. And every time he does that, he markets a product or service in that ezine. And he does this once a week, and it's not uncommon for him to sell anywhere between $2,000 and $10,000 each week of his products and services. And now that has translated into a six figure income.

© 2007 Shortcuts to Internet Millions, LLC - All Rights Reserved Worldwide

There is one client who decided to quit his lucrative corporate job in the world of health and fitness and go out and start an Internet site. He thought about joining the market of simply selling supplements to the masses, and then he did his research and thought about the competition he would be going up against.

So rather than sell health and fitness products to the masses, he began selling those items just to golfers. So now he is selling vitamins and supplements to golfers, and it is not uncommon for him to make $10,000, $15,000, $20,000 per month. Now he has moved on and is selling weight loss products. It is not uncommon for him to make anywhere from $50,000 to $200,000 a month by using the strategies in the books that you now have in your hands.

Another man I met several years ago started setting up websites back in the early to mid-1990's and it was when Netscape first came up with their browser. He was doing a lot of multi-media work, but he switched everything over to just trying to do whatever it took to generate sales on the Internet. His results can speak for themselves.

He's created a site that got one million hits, one million visitors without any funding, no big venture capital and kick-off party for this business. He just created the site and got one million visitors. From there, he just started consulting with clients, and this really led to him creating a lot of affiliate programs for his clients, kind of like Amazon.com has done. And what he discovered online is that very few people know how to generate leads and make sales. So he started creating training products that showed people exactly how to do that and how to increase their revenues on their Internet sites, and it was all based on the work he had done with clients. He showed them how to sell products and he began creating training systems to teach people how to put the Internet into plain English. Now he does public speaking, he creates products, he trains people, and he also consults with clients all over the world.

Now, all he did to learn to really succeed was he just continued to test things, and that's what we've asked you to do, try things out, see how they work for you. He evaluated his approach to every single on-line business he worked with and he ran it through the common sense approaches that you will read about in these books. And he tested small to see if things had a pulse, and when they did, he tested larger and larger.

Now interestingly enough, to build his business, the on-line approaches he uses most often are affiliate programs. His favorite on-line tools are auto-responders and email follow-up systems, and he also uses his database and his email software to really drive his entire business, but his favorite tool of all isn't actually on-line, it's the telephone. He actually picks it up and calls people. He thanks them for buying from him. When he came out with a new book, he actually called the first 1,000 people that bought to thank them personally, and this has actually helped skyrocket his business because nobody on the Internet is doing such things.

Chapter 2
Twenty-Five Lessons For Success and Six Things to Watch Out For

You want to imitate and try to improve on the success elements that have worked for others. You don't want to copy or steal from anybody else, but if you see something that's working, you want to creatively emulate it.

1. You'll notice that a lot of the successful Internet marketers are selling their own products. They may also be joint venturing and selling other people's, but they also have at least one of their own products or services where they keep all the money.

2. First of all find a market, but then find out what your market wants. You can do this through research, through surveys, and through reading other people's materials.

3. Pick a market that can afford to buy your product.

4. Create an affiliate program and market your programs through reseller and partner programs.

5. Test your marketing strategies, test your ads and your emails, your ezines and your auto-responders, and tweak them accordingly. It's necessary to get maximum response from them.

6. Email is probably the most effective on-line tool that you can use. Your list is the most valuable asset your business has.

7. Ezines. You must have or should have, or at least should test publishing an ezine. It may be the most profitable email that you ever send out.

8. It is advantageous to learn how to write good copy or else you need to hire someone.

9. The two-step approach is often the best route to go. And that is you generate leads and then you convert those leads to sales.

10. Follow-up is critical. Follow-up via auto-responders is the easiest.

11. You must have credibility and build trust wherever possible.

12. Internet marketing is emotional direct response marketing and is about building relationships.

13. Don't use the Internet to ignore your customers. Give them great customer service and you'll stand out above the competition.

14. Remember the lifetime value of a customer. If you treat them right and provide quality products, they will continue to buy from you over and over and over again so that they are worth a lot more than that very initial sale.

15. You want to make sure you diversify your on-line business. Don't just have one product and service. You need multiple products and services or you need to promote other people's products and services all based on a particular topic.

16. You may get your own domain name or license a turnkey website with its own domain name but don't use one of the free domain sites.

17. Cross-promoting and joint venturing with other websites is an effective marketing strategy.

18. You can build your subscriber list, credibility and name recognition by participating in newsgroups and discussion lists.

19. Endorsed emails pull better than ads, i.e. another person endorsing your product to their list will get a better response than just an ad in their ezine.

20. Only endorse quality products and services.

21. The tighter your niche is, the less competition you'll have.

22. Use the free PR techniques that you learned in our other books to generate traffic to your Internet site for low or no cost.

23. Even if you work out of your house, be professional.

24. Offering a freebie that has a high perceived value will often get you email names and subscribers. It's an effective marketing strategy proven again and again to work.

25. Automation is critical. It will save you time and hassles down the road.

Six Things to Watch Out For

1. Never spam or send UCE (unsolicited commercial email). It will cause you more trouble than it's worth.

2. Be careful about endorsing other people's products. You should buy the product or review the product ahead of time because it's your credibility at stake.

3. Focus. Try to minimize the time wasting distractions in your business and get to the job at hand. Work on your most important items first like marketing.

4. Experiment and test new things. Testing on-line is much cheaper, oftentimes almost zero cost.

5. Don't give up. Learn what you can from whatever you just tried and then move on.

6. Make computer back-ups especially of your most important files and your customer and email lists.

© 2007 Shortcuts to Internet Millions, LLC - All Rights Reserved Worldwide
www.BigLeaguePlayersClub.com

Chapter 3
Who Am I Going To Market to On-Line?

Everybody seems to take the wrong approach when they market on-line. They go out and decide "Well, this is what I'm going to market". They pick an affiliate program possibly, then they put up an Internet site, they start marketing, and then they're disappointed when they don't get any sales. Well see, the little known secret behind making money in any business is finding a market that wants something. So the real secret is to go out and find somebody that is already asking for something and then you find that something that they want and you give it to them. You may have heard this secret before. At this point, you've probably read it in other areas of our programs. So that's the real deal here. On the Internet it's all about finding traffic or creating it.

Now, what's the secret behind selecting the right markets or the right products and services to sell those markets that I found? Well, what you do is many people will say, "Find a need and fill it." And that might be one of the most misleading statements of all time. It had good intentions, however, what you want to do is you want to **find a want and fill it**. What you do is you find what they want, but you give them what they need. You sell them what they want, but you give them what they need. And that's really what it is. That's the bottom line. It's very simple, but it's very, very powerful. <u>There are other things to think about, but what you do is find out what they want and you give it to them.</u>

Okay, so remember the sequence.

1. First is, find out what they want
2. Go find the products and services that fill that want.
3. Make sure they can afford to buy what you're offering

So, you want to determine that ahead of time. It's very important to do it in this order, and also you want to make sure they can afford to buy what you're offering. It's no good finding out that they want something and finding a product and service, but then finding out that they can't afford it.

Market Research to Find a Market

What you need to do is constantly review places on the Internet. You need to be reading the news and reading ezines and trying to figure out the goals that people are striving for and the problems they are trying to avoid.

Market research really is just a process of finding out what they really want, like we mentioned before, because then we'll help them achieve it. And if there are things they want to avoid, we'll give them products and services that will help them avoid those things.

So, when you are constantly open and looking for this type of information, you will find out things like:

© 2007 Shortcuts to Internet Millions, LLC - All Rights Reserved Worldwide
www.BigLeaguePlayersClub.com

- Which subjects are most popular and profitable
- Which items have the most likelihood of success based on hungry markets that are available
- How to improve current products or services so that you will now have something new to sell to a market that's already buying things
- What angle to take or hot buttons to push to reach your typical prospect
- Problems and concerns and questions your prospects have and that you need to address or need to solve in your marketing
- What they don't like about certain products and services and then you can change them
- You'll figure out things that you should ignore or avoid

Market research really is not hard to do and it will give you great insight and be one of the most valuable things you can do.

Depending on your situation, you can conduct market research in a couple of different areas. One you can do broad research where you are looking at different fields and different subject areas and you might decide on something that's profitable to build a business around even though you're not in that industry now. Or you might decide to build a popular business around a particular trend that's going on in our society. And you can possibly even adapt what you are currently doing to ride along on that current trend. Another way is to do research within your existing industry. You can conduct research and find out better what people in your current industry really want. Most people ignore their customers, and if you do constant market research, you'll be able to keep on the cusp of what your market wants and continually innovate ahead of your competition.

Now the way to do research on-line is to go out to your search engines and look for the "top 100 websites", or look for the most popular websites, or search for "best seller lists", or search for "top 100 downloads", and you'll see what people are actually doing on the Internet, and there's no better research than seeing what people are actually doing. And when these lists don't really fit in your particular industry, you'll still be able to understand what people are thinking and what they are wanting and you'll be able to translate those possibly to your own industry, if not, then you can just continue looking until you find enough information. But by studying what's working for other top businesses in your field and in other fields, you'll find out enough information to adapt to your own business.

You can run surveys or run contests or do little popularity type tests and find out and weigh one subject against another. For example, say you were going to create an information product and you want to know which one has the best potential for sales. With a very little bit of investment, you could write several small reports that are about those topics. Now to determine which one is more popular, you can give them away free on-line, or you can run classified ads or run smaller ads in ezines, or write articles about them. You can actually write the same article that was generic enough, but at the end one time you gave one free report and the next time you run the article you give the other free report. And if you keep good records, you'll all of a sudden

© 2007 Shortcuts to Internet Millions, LLC - All Rights Reserved Worldwide

see which report was being downloaded or being requested more often, and that would give you an idea which route to go.

You can adapt this and use it in a lot of different ways to test and do research very inexpensively. If you pay very close attention to your feedback and the questions and comments people make, you'll really be pointed in the right direction as far as what idea you should pick over the other one. You'll find out what problems they want solved, what concerns or worries they have, and they'll tell you all kinds of things. So if you can come up with a product or service that then offers solutions to those problems and questions they have, then you may be starting out on a winner.

If you continue to follow this plan, almost all of your ideas will be at least profitable, some more so than others. You can encourage this feedback from people by doing surveys, by email, or through forms on your Internet site, and just simply either make your email address available for them to reply to or have them click on a submit button and your feedback will be on its way. Be sure you keep all of this feedback just in case it doesn't fit into what you're doing now and you go on to create something else, you may come back later on and still use that research and those articles for a future product.

Next, we want to see what's already selling on the Internet. And some things are just a natural fit.

Information products, which you've been taught elsewhere in this material, are a great fit to sell on the Internet. Keep in mind that certain things can still be adapted to and sold virtually in almost any category.

For example, you can sell software, information products, Internet services, and advertising. Those can be sold in any niche. And, almost anything that can be successfully sold off-line, can pretty much be successfully sold on-line too with some adaptation.

Of course, there's no guarantee of success if you happen to select one of the categories I'm about to give you and it doesn't work on-line, things change and trends change very quickly on the Internet. But these things are currently working and are currently being sold on-line, and we'll just give you a couple of categories:

- **Communities.** One thing that is being sold on the Internet is communities. They are being built around topics such as Internet marketing, copywriting, fitness, buying and selling real estate, websites, antiques, press releases, beauty products, kitchen aids, automobiles, golf and self-defense. These things are all niches that you could go into and you could sell books, videos and audiotapes, and other courses in on-line chat rooms and things like that, and build basically a community around these types of things.
- **Automotive accessories**
- **Income opportunities**

© 2007 Shortcuts to Internet Millions, LLC - All Rights Reserved Worldwide
www.BigLeaguePlayersClub.com

Collectibles
- Antiques
- Books
- Coins
- Stamps
- Computer hardware
- Software
- Computer training and programming

Consumer goods
- Clothing
- Electronics
- Flowers
- Gourmet specialty foods

Entertainment category
- Event tickets
- Music

Financial category
- Stocks
- Bonds
- All kinds of investment vehicles

The information category
- Audiocassettes
- Booklets
- Books
- CD-ROMS
- Consulting
- Newsletters
- Seminars
- Videos

Health and beauty category
- Cosmetics
- Exercise equipment
- Herbs

Other
- Give away free stuff sites like CGI programs, game sites and business software sites that give away demos
- Award sites
- Consumer report sites
- News sites that are free, but they usually try to drive a lot of traffic to their site and then charge people for advertising

© 2007 Shortcuts to Internet Millions, LLC - All Rights Reserved Worldwide
www.BigLeaguePlayersClub.com

- Web design and search engine positioning
- Banner design
- Internet press releases
- Classified ad submissions

Travel category
- Airline tickets
- Car rentals
- Lodging

Sports
- Sports news
- Sports equipment
- Nutritional products

Exclusive Products

Now when you look at most people marketing on the Internet, they are marketing at least one product of their own, or oftentimes more than that.

They might also market other people's affiliate programs, but they want to market their own too. The reason is the higher profits; you get to keep them all, 100% of yours versus maybe only 40 to 50% if you're selling somebody else's.

There are better back-end profits. Back-end profits are defined as the follow-up sales you make to someone that you made an initial sale to. Now that someone's already purchased from you, the back-end sales are worth so much more because you get to keep all of the profit and the advertising cost is next to zero. You are in a better position to create back-end sales when the first purchase is one of your own.

A common problem is that people go on the Internet and they join a ton of affiliate programs and they don't even have their own website. So it's good to have your own site promoting a product from that site, and then when you build that list you can refer people to suppliers of other products, and other affiliate programs.

How to Develop or Acquire Your Own Product

1. Simply make the product yourself. Now a lot of people don't think they can create their own products. They don't think they are creative enough, or they think it's going to take too long, or they just never get around to doing it. They are always getting ready to get ready. And product creation does take more effort than going out and getting the rights to a product from someone else, but the rewards can far outweigh the challenge of creating a product.

2. Hire someone to create the product for you. And we have resources on where you can find people to create products for you. If you want to hire someone to create

© 2007 Shortcuts to Internet Millions, LLC - All Rights Reserved Worldwide

products for you, it's really best to have an agreement with them that you get exclusive rights to that product. In other words, they are performing a "work for hire".

3. Team up with someone else to create products and maybe the partner has certain skills, education and assets that they can bring to the venture that you might not have. So you might be able to interview someone else for instance and create a brand new tape product.

4. You can license the rights to somebody else's product. There are tons and tons of books that can be turned into courses where those books have never seen the light of day. You can go to the library and look into a publication called "Books In Print" and look up the authors. Most of these books never make bookstores. We know of one client that simply bought the rights to a book that had sold well in mail order ads over and over and over again, so he purchased the rights for the book actually from the daughter of the deceased author, and rewrote some of it, improved of it, and it continues to sell well to this day on the Internet.

How to Acquire Exclusive Product Rights

Now getting exclusive rights to a product can be very good also, not only for your own products obviously, but for products of other people. Here are some options you have:

1. Copyright. Copyright laws cover your intellectual property and your printed information, software and sculptures, and they are international in scope so they give the creator the exclusive rights to sell their work for a lifetime. So, those rights also transfer to the creator's family for what might be 50 to 75 years beyond the author's life. I think currently anything from 1922 and before you can pretty much use but you should consult a good copyright lawyer.

2. Patents. Coming up with a unique patent invention is another way where you have exclusive rights. These are a little more difficult and it's also more expensive and a lot harder for most people to do.

3. Go straight to the source. Whoever has rights to the product you should try to negotiate exclusive marketing rights from them and depending on what you arrange, you might have the absolute sole right to promote this product on the Internet, for instance. Or you might have certain distribution channels or certain languages or certain geographic areas. You never know what you're going to get until you talk to the primary source. We've actually gone out and acquired the rights to books and courses and other things, and we are currently negotiating and trying to get the mail order rights to a product that has sold well on television, but it has only sold on television. So once we start promoting it through the mail, we expect it to be successful also. We'll be the only ones that have the rights to sell it through the mail.

4. Go to the library and look at old newsletters and old books in print editions and find old products and services that have been lying dormant. There are tons and tons of things that sold in the '60's, '70's, '80's and '90's, and even before, that was just as relevant in

© 2007 Shortcuts to Internet Millions, LLC - All Rights Reserved Worldwide
www.BigLeaguePlayersClub.com

those days as it is now. Some of those products just simply need to be updated, and some don't even need to be updated. So, that's another way to get products.

5. You can also just run ads. "Do you have an idea for a product? I'm a marketing expert. If you're an author, inventor, vendor, manufacturer, or importer of unique, hard to find products that you think would be a hot seller with the right marketing help, let me help you." Then give your contact information.

Reselling Products and Services of Others Through Licensing

Even though marketing your own products and services has a lot of benefits, there are a lot of good reasons to license and promote other people's products and services too. Earlier we talked about diversifying and expanding your offerings so you'll have a variety of things to offer your customers and, in one of the other books, we talk about how to build an affiliate program and how to utilize other people's affiliate programs. So, you still need to identify the wants and the needs within your market and try to develop your own products, but from time to time, if you're doing that well and creating a good relationship from time to time you can license and promote the products and services of other people that are attracted to your subscriber list or your customer list. When you license and promote the goods of others and you have a good relationship, they really take your advice and you're in a position where you can **suggest** ideas and things to them, rather than seem like you're cramming them down their throat.

Now, there are various ways you can resell products of other people. You can purchase and stock inventory. You can buy things from them and actually stock it if you have that kind of space, but then you're investing in inventory and you're hoping you can still sell them. You can also arrange drop shipping by suppliers. And with drop shipping, you're just the middleman, you promote, place and get orders on the Internet and then you have somebody ship it. One associate of ours was actually selling diamonds on the Internet. Now he did not have his own jewelry store or his own vault of diamonds. He simply had the Internet, sold the diamonds, and then the wholesalers took care of supplying the diamonds.

Your customers pay you for products upfront when you are selling them something on the Internet. You then actually forward the orders onto whoever, the discount warehouse or the dealer that you're getting information from, you forward the information to them and they ship it out. They also can have preprinted mailing labels with your information on them so that they can put those on there and it still looks like it's being shipped from you. And then the difference between what you have to pay them for the item and the item you charged is your profit. And the drop ship method is very convenient for a lot of people and it's a lot less risky than having a whole bunch of inventory, because if you don't make any sales, then you just don't make any profit, but you haven't laid out any money to stock inventory.

Another way is to simply refer a person to the prime source who has the product and they take over from there. They use their sales methods and everything. This sometimes is like an affiliate program.

© 2007 Shortcuts to Internet Millions, LLC - All Rights Reserved Worldwide
www.BigLeaguePlayersClub.com

So you set up a site and you drive traffic to the main site and let them do the selling, and you collect the checks. This is really the most popular type of joint venture on the Internet today, and it's the easiest to implement. The cost to join is almost always free and you can make upward of anywhere between 20 and 75% of the sales price. Now the methods vary somewhat, but generally each partner is given their own unique website URL or <u>U</u>nique <u>R</u>esource <u>L</u>ocator and it links to the original website and they have software that tracks your unique code so that it knows to pay you commissions. What happens is the partners just promote the products and services, they direct the traffic to the appropriate website with their special code and when that visitor goes there and it results in a sale, then you earn a commission. Once you refer the prospect to that website, through your unique ID, then that company takes over. They might send out emails to follow-up, but they process the order, they collect payments, ship products, they do all the services and support, they track the sales and then they credit you and mail out your commission check.

Now depending on the type, sometimes there is what's called the "two-tier" program where you can make money on two levels, but you can learn all about that in the Website Sales Force book.

Finding a Product or Service Without an Affiliate Program

Every once in a while, you might find something that you'd like to test market, but they don't really have an affiliate program, they're just selling it, or maybe it's not even on the Internet and you find it and want to test market by selling it via the Internet. Then you just go straight to the supplier and ask if they'll drop ship it. At that point, you might risk a little bit of an investment and get a small amount of inventory, and then if you do your marketing test and it proves to be a good seller, you can either invest in more inventory or set up the drop shipping with the vendor.

Why Information Marketing and the Internet Are Perfect For Each Other

The absolute ideal product for the Internet is an information product.

Even as much as information as there is available on-line, which actually just continues to increase daily, there are still people out there that want to buy valuable information products that will help them solve their problems and help them reach their goals.

In a way, all the information out there that is cluttering the Internet, kind of creates even a better market. See, people don't know where to look, they don't know what to read, they don't know what quality is, so if you bring pieces of information together and can skillfully craft it into a product, and then it will save them time from trying to gather this information from all over the place.

Plus there is great profit potential in quality information products, and there are a lot of good reasons that information marketing really goes well with the Internet.

1. Internet users are oftentimes info junkies. They are always looking for information on-line, that's one of the main uses of the Internet.
2. There is a large percentage of Internet business owners are already providing information in at least one shape or form.
3. Providing free information to people in hopes that they'll give you their email address or subsequently return and buy something is a tried and true information Internet marketing strategy. You offer free information and it builds a large list of ezine subscribers or you offer free information on your website and it attracts a lot of visitors and then you can sell advertising.

By building up a loyal audience that really is eager to see your new information, you'll have access to valuable prospects that you can reach over and over again.

On the Internet, you can actually expand the size of your audience. It's virtually limitless.

You can have repeat contact with them over and over again on little to no cost because you are just sending out emails. Now staying in touch with prospects in a mail order business includes the cost of mailing newsletters and envelopes and postage and so on. Now, you don't have to give away everything, but giving away a little bit of information for free, that can create something called reciprocity where the person on the other end feels obligated to reciprocate or buy, and on the Internet, giving away something for free is virtually cost free.

In fact, on the Internet, you can also get paid for things you already have. You can have audio tapes transcribed into booklets, you can have videotapes transcribed or recorded into audio files and you might as well get paid for things you already have, so you create something just once and you can use it over and over again.

When the valuable information you publish is actually your own, your credibility and position as an expert in your field increases. Credibility is of paramount importance on the Internet. You also can use some of your information to generate free publicity without spending any money on advertising. You can distribute articles to other webmasters, you can get things printed in other ezines and these will all generate traffic and publicity for your website.

Ebooks Are All the Rage

Having freebies on your Internet site oftentimes is a good marketing strategy and a lot of people are giving out free ebooks.

What they are doing is compiling a bunch of articles or they're writing a summary of what their product is and they're turning them into electronic books, or what is called ebooks.

The advantage is you don't have to have it typeset and printed. If you publish it on-line, there are no printing costs. The distribution costs are next to nothing. You can also update this information when it's in electronic format and you don't have to worry about printing and

© 2007 Shortcuts to Internet Millions, LLC - All Rights Reserved Worldwide

keeping them in inventory. It starts becoming updated from the very next download. And ebooks can be given away. They are great lead generators. They make great bonuses. They make great freebies to build your ezine subscription list. And they are great items to help generate traffic to your website.

© 2007 Shortcuts to Internet Millions, LLC - All Rights Reserved Worldwide
www.BigLeaguePlayersClub.com

Chapter 4
Getting Your Internet Business Set Up

This section will help you avoid problems when getting your Internet business up and on-line.

Even if you're already established, there might be some useful information in this chapter that will help you get more organized. The best way to get organized and become more efficient is having the right tools and to get the right tools for your Internet business.

Things You Must Consider When Picking a Web Host

Since where your website resides is extremely important to your ability to market it, the things that we are going to talk about here are very important. You want to consider these things when selecting a host. You need to consider your monthly fees, it's not always the most important thing, but you don't want to be throwing away a ton of money, and you don't want to be going for such a cheap hosting fee that you're not getting good quality. You can pay anywhere from $14.95 - $59.95 for good hosting of JUST ONE site - from no support on the low end to 24 by 7 support on the high end.

Just as an explanation, ISP's and hosting companies generally are two different companies You might have an ISP where, in other words, you're connecting to the Internet through your local cable company, if you have a cable modem, or you're using America Online®. But you're using some company that could be located in New York City or in San Francisco or in Oregon that might have rooms and rooms full of servers that actually will host your Internet site. And they have back-up servers and they are connected to what's called the backbone of the Internet so that your communications can be reached from all over the world. So, it's quite possible and probable that you will have an ISP, which helps you connect to the Internet and then you will host your websites at a different company.

Customer Support

24 by 7 live support can be very expensive. Some live support at the very minimum would be nice. But the norm is simply email support.

As far as replies to email support, you should get response in a couple hours during business hours and at least within 24 hours when you send them in the middle of the night.

The best kind of support it would seem is 24 hours a day, 365 days a year, live phone support. However, it is also the most expensive. We've often found that we haven't needed support from our hosting company for weeks and months at a time. So, as long as we can send them an email and get a response within a few hours, or if it's after hours by the next morning, that's usually sufficient.

So that's probably what you should look for in customer support.

© 2007 Shortcuts to Internet Millions, LLC - All Rights Reserved Worldwide
www.BigLeaguePlayersClub.com

Other Features

Auto-responders. Auto-responders are an added marketing tool that's offered with some hosting plans. Smart auto-responders are even better. And those are the ones that allow you to merge personal information into the emails that you send out. With the hosting package we've put together for you, they include this software on the Internet sites that you get from them.

You also want a secure ordering capability and the ability to accept credit cards on-line because if secure ordering is not available, your sales will drop off drastically.

Website Statistics

You want to be able to get your web stats because this will tell you how many people are coming to your website, how many pages they're looking at, where they're coming from, what browsers they are using, and how long they're staying. All of these things can be important in determining what you should do with your websites. So you want to make sure that you have good statistics that have log files that give you daily, weekly and monthly statistics.

CGI Programs

You also want to have what's called CGI program ability. That means you can put custom little programs on your website like discussion boards and guest books and survey forms and all kinds of little scripts that you can get that will help you out with search engines and all kinds of neat little features that you might want to add for your customers. So you need the ability to install CGI programs.

FrontPage Extensions

You also want Front Page extensions to be available. This will allow you to use Microsoft's FrontPage® product, which allows you to create Internet sites almost just as easy as if you were using Microsoft Word®.

Database Availability

You also want to look to see if you have the ability to have databases on your website just in case you need them for larger projects, or creating membership sites, etc. Most times you won't need a database, but you would like the availability to be there.

And finally, just a couple of other things you want. Password security is important so that you can secure certain areas of your website. You want to have email aliases so that you can create an email such as sales@yoursite.com or info@yoursite.com. You also want what's called "pop" email accounts so that different people in your organization can have their own email address. So these are the things that you want and we have created relationships with hosting companies that will provide all of these things to you at a very, very comparable price, if not lower than most.

Designing Your Internet Site for Profitability

Most designers create a site from a cosmetic standpoint. They like the way it looks and it's like Madison Avenue advertising. It's almost as if they're trying to win awards. So, if you're going to let someone else design it, the information you are about to read will be useful and you need to make sure that they follow these instructions.

The first step in planning your Internet site is being aware of what you're trying to accomplish. And if making money is the absolute ultimate goal of your site, then we need to follow some steps. Now building traffic to your site is important, yes. But it's what you do with that traffic that really counts. It doesn't matter if your site gets a million visitors a month, if you don't convert any of them to paying customers or even convince them to leave their email addresses, then you're not going to make enough money to pay your hosting fees.

It would be nice if every visitor that came to your site did something and it resulted in a sale the first time they came. But there are some real statistics about the Internet that a lot of people don't' know about.

1. Many people don't buy on the first visit
2. Many people never visit a site after their initial visit
3. Only a very small percentage of website visits actually result in an action being taken, either an email address being given or a sale being made.

The Number One Goal of Your Internet Site

With these above facts in mind, we have to realize that there are a couple of things we need that are very important.

One is your site needs to promote some kind of repeat contact, in other words, visitors need to know that they're going to be contacted again, so you need to get their email address.

Two, your website really needs to do a good job of selling whatever it is supposed to sell, so it needs to get a certain percentage of those visitors to take action, which is to either download a free trial, buy something or whatever. So let's look at these goals a little bit closer.

Promoting repeat contact, letting them know that you're going to be in touch with them again and there is a variety of reasons that visitors never come back:

1. It's not easy
2. There is nothing on the site that gathers email information or any other personal information from these people that can be used to encourage them to come back again
3. Visitors don't find anything of interest that would make them want to come back
4. They find something that they don't like. They find something distasteful or find something that they just don't like about your site.

© 2007 Shortcuts to Internet Millions, LLC - All Rights Reserved Worldwide
www.BigLeaguePlayersClub.com

Now the great thing is we can address these situations.

#1 Let's make it easy for them to return to our site. Two things really stop this; one is that the domain name is hard to remember. Now you can try to make it easier by selecting a good, easy domain name that's easy to remember, but it's getting harder and harder because a lot of good domain names are already taken. Or you can make sure you license programs that already have good domain names which some licensing programs do. All you really need is a phrase that someone can remember. A test that we use is if you can leave the website name on an answering machine and people would be able to still understand it, then it is o.k. Thus, we can call up someone and say, "Hey, come on out to **http://www.BigLeaguePlayersClub.com**" and chances are they're going to spell that right and they're going to be able to get there, even though that's kind of a long domain name.

Now, not having anything in place to gather information that can then be used to encourage them to come back, well we can solve this by starting right from the get-go to try to collect or try to get the visitors to volunteer information. It's so important to get them back that you need to begin this right away. So, we need to get them, at the minimum, to leave their email address. Next, it would be nice if they left their first name so we can merge that in emails we send to them.

In almost all Internet businesses, the email is the most important item to gather because of these four reasons. One is email is extremely inexpensive. There is no printing and postage or phone calls or faxing. You can go out to thousands and thousands of people for next to nothing.

So we need to get their email address.

#2 You can reach large numbers of subscribers without using spam since they actually have given you their email address and they're on your list.

#3 You can remind them to come back to your site and you can also offer other products and services right in those emails or ezines, as you've learned in one of our other companion books.

#4 Your website is just sitting there and it's waiting for visitors, so you need to do something. You need to drive traffic there with search engines or with joint ventures. But with email, it doesn't just sit there, it actually goes out to your potential visitors and takes the message right to their inbox instead of like the website, it waits for them to go there and read the message.

You have to understand that prospects are very busy and they're doing a lot of other things. So if you leave it up to them to come back to your website, it ain't going to happen.

So you need to invite them to come back. You need to invite them to leave their email address and that way you are basically telling them, "Hey, I am going to be contacting you again." And then you'll have a much better chance of getting them to come back to your site or getting them to perform some kind of action. And don't attempt to get their information in just one area.

© 2007 Shortcuts to Internet Millions, LLC - All Rights Reserved Worldwide
www.BigLeaguePlayersClub.com

We put forms that ask for email addresses on almost every page of our website. Sometimes we don't put it on order pages because we don't want to distract from an order, however, on all of our main pages, we usually have what's called an opt-in form where the visitor opts to give us their email address. We want to give them several opportunities and then, of course, there are various ways to use email to build that repeat website traffic. You send out ezines or other periodic emails that then have links that bring them back to the website. You also can use auto-responders and that will build repeat traffic. You can subscribe them to a series of emails that are provided through your auto-responder service. And then it's just done and it periodically sends them the next email in the sequence.

Now the next problem was making your site interesting enough so that they'll want to come back. Well, sometimes your site may just simply be a site that sells something. It might just look like a sales letter and have an order form. But giving a visitor other reasons to come back if you are selling multiple products, then there are things you probably need to do.

You might want to make the site include articles and different types of free information; Now one thing a lot of Internet users have in common is they are all info junkies, so if you give really valuable free information, then people will come out to your site and people will tell other people about your site.

Another way to encourage people to come back is to have a discussion board or chat room so that people are coming back and posting questions and talking to each other, etc., and you'll benefit from this traffic. The one thing you have to watch out for is you can create a discussion board and there can be a lot of negative buzz. On our discussion boards, we actually keep them in a member password protected area where only members that pay us to access our site and our private areas get to use our discussion boards. Some other Internet marketers we know actually have public discussion boards and they let people put anything they want out there, and oftentimes people start slamming other people and we just don't want to get involved in that. But that is an option and when you do that all you have to do is put a disclaimer on there that the views of those people aren't necessarily the discussion board owners. However, you would want to consult a competent attorney to make sure that you couldn't get in trouble for comments made by other people on your discussion board.

Now the final problem is we want to try to avoid visitors finding things that they don't like about our website. Now, **slow loading pages are just about the number one turnoff**, especially these days when people's modems are a little bit faster than they used to be, a lot of people have cable and DSL access, so you need to have very quick loading pages. They need to load in 10 seconds or less, and the way to do that is to just create simple web pages with just text and maybe some small graphics. Even those graphics should be compressed.

It's quite well known within Internet marketing circles that plain looking sites actually earn a higher profit than the fancy ones. The important thing is really what you say at your website, it's not how many flashing lights and twirling whizzygigs you have. So the primary objective when you design a site that's going to make money is not to make it razzle dazzle, but to make it a powerful selling tool that visitors can use and they want to order from.

© 2007 Shortcuts to Internet Millions, LLC - All Rights Reserved Worldwide
www.BigLeaguePlayersClub.com

It doesn't mean you don't want to make it look good, but that's not of primary importance. A general guideline is you want a page to load in 10 seconds or less, including all the graphics and that will mean it needs to be 50 to 60K or less in size. And you might only want 4 to 5 images per page on your site. If you have duplicates of one image, that really counts as one because it's going to be just loading one copy of that graphic, and if you add up all of those graphics, you want to still try to keep the size of your page within the 50 to 60k limit.

If you end up with a very large graphic that you really need for your presentation, you can display what's called a thumbnail version, which is a smaller version that someone will see, and if they really want to see the larger one, they click on it and you can even put a little message next to it that says, "Click here to enlarge" and what that does is that links to a page that has a larger picture of the item, and that saves you size on your primary page.

Also, you have something in your html code that you'll want to make sure you utilize and that is the ALT tags. What this does is if you specify the size of your images in the ALT tags, it lets the browser start loading the text right away and it allows the visitors to see that text while the graphics are then loading because the site knows what size those graphics are. If you leave the size off, then it has to figure out where everything is going to go on the whole page and it loads slowly. Another trick is to create what's called a TABLE. You create a TABLE at the top of your website and put about a screen's worth of stuff in that TABLE, and then create a second TABLE below that where you put the rest of your website, that way the initial table will load and they will have something to look at while the rest of your Internet site is actually loading.

Now when putting a lot of text on your website, you want to make the text visually appealing, you don't want it to be real intimidating, so you need to avoid having endless streams of large blocks of text. You want to use smaller bits of text and a white space in between to make it a little easier on the eyes. And black, dark blue on white or maybe on beige or on off white background, these work the best. So regardless of color combinations, you just don't want visitors to be looking at your website and straining their eyes.

The next point is you want to make key points stand out by using bold or contrasting colors, not necessarily sharp contrasting colors, but bold contrasting colors. In other words, if you have a bulleted list of items, you might want to bold every other item. You can use italics, although they're not as easy to see on-line. Bulleted lists again are good. Underlining things on the Internet may confuse people and it may make them think that they need to click on those items. So you may want to avoid using underlines on your Internet sites unless it's an actual link.

Don't use more than two or three fonts per web page and a very proven combination on-line is using Arial or Helvetica for headlines and subheadings, and then the body copy itself is Times New Roman or Verdana.

Now remember also that fonts available on a visitor's computer will determine what they see. So if you use some odd fonts or little known fonts and they're not available on your user's computer, you may not have any idea what it's going to look like.

© 2007 Shortcuts to Internet Millions, LLC - All Rights Reserved Worldwide
www.BigLeaguePlayersClub.com

You want to check your site for typographic and grammatical errors, very poorly written words and very badly misspelled words can lower your credibility. It might hinder people from coming back, so have them spell checked. Have somebody else review them. If the way you write is very hard for people to understand, they may not come back. So again, if you just absolutely can't get the writing done, you may need to have somebody else edit your material.

Now, if the navigation around your site is difficult, they also might not come back. So you want to organize your links in a very attractive and organized way so that visitors can go from one place to another place with a minimum amount of clicks. They don't want to have to click 100 times to get somewhere.

Another very poorly designed thing that you can have on a website is when the page loads, it is so wide that your user has to use a scrollbar to go left and right to see the whole screen. It's very much of a drag to have to go back and forth on each line that you're reading, so you want to design your site so this doesn't happen.

You want to make sure that your website can be read in older browsers. So if you're always writing your web pages to take advantage of just the latest cutting-edge technology, you're going to run into problems because a lot of people use the same old browsers year in and year out and those old browsers aren't compatible to new technologies.

Don't use frames. Although frames are used on a lot of sites, they're awkward to navigate, they're confusing to people, the search engines don't like them, they have problems indexing them which means your free traffic from search engines may never appear. But it really needs to be based on how important search engine ranking is to you. If the search engine ranking doesn't matter because you are doing things in a different manner, then frames maybe absolutely fine for you and if the use of frames does not create a confusing situation for your visitors, then it's probably okay, and as mentioned before, browser compatibility. You want to make sure you write your web pages for all versions of Internet Explorer and Netscape for the most part. Those are going to get most of your visitors. And you want to go back to maybe Internet 3.0 and Netscape 3.0, maybe 4.0 at this point. That would be sufficient.

You want to avoid html programming errors, so if people bring up your web page and errors pop up and they see boxes pop up that say there's an error, there's going to be a problem. You need to view your pages in different types of browsers so you can make sure there aren't errors in other types of browsers. A common mistake is to create a web page and only view it in a browser that you have.

Another problem is inconvenient ordering methods. If you make it hard for your customers to order from you and in fact, you are selling something from the Internet and the only way they can order it is if they mail in a check, as you can see just like in mail order, that would be a problem and you would lose a lot of sales. So you want to make it as easy as possible, and on the Internet, you can get a merchant account and get it hooked up to your website and you can take advantage of accepting all the credit cards and checks and accepting those orders through a secure on-line form and the money is then deposited right into your bank. So you want to give

© 2007 Shortcuts to Internet Millions, LLC - All Rights Reserved Worldwide
www.BigLeaguePlayersClub.com

your customers a full variety of payment options. You also want to give them the option to send those orders in by check or by fax or by money order, or even by phone if possible.

How to Check Your Web Pages for Errors and Browser Compatibility

We mentioned earlier that this was one of the things that you need to pay attention to because your web pages can look completely different in a Netscape browser versus an Internet Explorer browser. Also, you might have things in your code that will actually cause errors depending on the type of browser.

So, you need to verify that things look the same from browser to browser and you don't get errors from browser to browser. There are things like the monitor size, screen resolution and other system configurations that a user can change on their computer that can affect the way web pages look. The worst thing about all these possible problems that might occur is because your web pages might look fine on your computer, you might be unaware of the adverse affects a bad looking web page might have on your website traffic, and you'll just think that's the traffic you're getting, but you won't know it's because you have a brand new web browser and no one with a prior release can look at your pages. So, you can be losing a lot of visitors that way. So never assume that it looks good, you need to check it in other browsers.

Websites should be designed to look good in Internet Explorer and Netscape, those are the two most common, and you usually should go back at least two versions. So of the writing at this current period in time, that would be Internet version 4.0 and Netscape 4.0. But you can keep up-to-date with that by coming out to our website.

Here are some strategies to help you find any potential problems with your website.

- If you have multiple computers available, check out your website on the different computers
- Have a list of friends that can log on from different types of computers and check out your site for you
- If you can go to a computer store or a library, you can check them out there
- If you find that you need improvements, one approach is to make adjustments on a test page, in other words, copy one of your main pages that might have problems and rename it
- Once you get it corrected and looking proper on that page and you make sure it's compatible, then you can just swap it out and also use it as a template.

E-Commerce

All right, now I want to talk about e-commerce. If your Internet business does require collecting payments from customers, which most of them do, then convenience is what you have to provide for your customers because if you make it hard for them to buy, they're just going to click away because they're too busy and they can move on to another website. So the minute it becomes a hassle whatsoever, you've lost them.

© 2007 Shortcuts to Internet Millions, LLC - All Rights Reserved Worldwide
www.BigLeaguePlayersClub.com

With that in mind, you want to be able to accept payments by checks, money orders, credit cards, bank debit; you should give them all these options. You can also allow them to submit through secure order forms and unsecured order forms through email, even by phone 24 hours toll-free if you can afford it and if your situation should require it. You should give them a fax number so they can fax in their orders. All of these items.

The benefits of accepting major credit cards are:

- ✓ Everybody buys with them. Our society is conditioned to buy with them
- ✓ Your profits will go up if you accept credit cards and conversely, your profits will go down if you do not accept credit cards
- ✓ They can give you instant credibility. It shows that you were able to get a merchant account and that you are a real business. And again, it gives them convenience
- ✓ They don't have to look for an envelope, they don't have to write a check, they don't have to find a stamp, they can just pay immediately
- ✓ It works off of their greed glands, in other words, they're ready to buy right now and if you accept credit cards, they'll click and buy
- ✓ It also increases service and fulfillment. There is no need for them to wait until the office opens the next day to call and order something. They can order in the middle of the night

So the bottom line is you must accept credit cards.

Secure Order Forms

There's been a lot of misinformation spread around about on-line credit card fraud and on-line credit card security. Theft does occur, don't get me wrong. But the level of risk has really been exaggerated and we don't know if that will ever go away. But there are still a lot of people that are uneasy about putting their credit card numbers on-line when they buy, so regardless of what the risk is, the perception is there. So you have to make them feel as secure as possible. And in doing that, one way to do that is to provide a secure order form, what's called an "encrypted SSL technology" and this scrambles the data that the customer puts in and makes it inaccessible by thieves. And of all the ordering options that we offer, check, cash, money order, Visa, MasterCard, American Express, mailing in, faxing in, phoning in, emailing in or secure order form, most of the sales come through the secure order form. So, we get more profit by having that secure on-line credit card option. And if we didn't have secure order forms available, we know we would lose sales. It's that simple. Some people would order through the non-secure form, some would mail and call, but some would simply say forget about it and go away.

Real-Time Credit Card Processing

Here's how real-time credit card processing works. The customer comes to your site and places an order using your secure order form. That information is actually sent through a gateway to the bank clearing house and within seconds it's authorized and your website is notified. If declined, the order doesn't go through. If approved, it goes through. And then the funds are usually put into your bank account within 2 to 3 days.

Checks by Fax, Phone, Email and Web-Based Forms

Now with this method, this allows a customer to pay with a check, and many people like to pay with business checks. They don't have credit cards or they don't like to pay with credit cards, so they want to use a checking account.

What they do is actually submit their checking account data, the routing number for their bank and their account number, bank name and so on, and they transmit this information to you either by faxing it to you or calling it in or entering it in a web form and submitting it to you. Then you can actually buy software that will allow you to buy check paper and print out checks that look just like normal checks and deposit them into your account or you can enter the checking information right into your online merchant account that we set up for you.

You also might want to hold off shipping products until these checks clear. Fortunately bounced checks don't happen that often, on the downside though, you have to delay order fulfillment, which might discourage some customers from doing business with you.

Other On-Line Payment Options

There are other on-line payment systems also, but a lot of them haven't caught on that well and some of them are quite bulky to use; "Paypal", you can run products through "Click Bank". Many of these systems are used for auctions; some take a large percentage of the profit. So, you really want to stick to getting your own merchant account. In fact, if you're going to be in business for yourself, you need a merchant account and that's all there is to it.

© 2007 Shortcuts to Internet Millions, LLC - All Rights Reserved Worldwide
www.BigLeaguePlayersClub.com

Chapter 5
Running Your Day-To-Day Internet Business

Give Great Customer Service

Many business owners today actually get upset when customers call or email. I'll give you an example. I was at my mechanics the other day and while I was at the counter, the phone was ringing off the hook, and every time the phone rang, the person answering the phone would shake their head in disgust and say, "Geez, these people, they won't leave me alone." Now, it seems to me that the phone ringing off the hook with interested customers or prospects wanting to come into your store to make appointments is a good thing. However, they treated the thought of the person calling with disgust.

Well, excellent customer service is going to help you profit over and over from these loyal customers. You'll get positive word of mouth and your company will become more credible. Now here are ways to deliver great customer service.

✓ Make the ordering process simple. The easier it is for the customer to enter the information and click "order" the better. You should ask for the minimum information that you need; that may be name, address, credit card, and expiration date.

✓ Make your website easy to get around. Don't make it hard for people to find the information they need. It should be one, two, three clicks away.

✓ Give simple ordering directions. Don't leave anything up to guesswork. Tell them exactly what to fill in and tell them exactly what to do. Do their thinking for them and give them complete details.

✓ Use a well-designed order form. In addition to giving them a secure order form and a way to accept credit cards, give them optional ways so that they can fax or print or copy the information into an email.

✓ Give them a FAQ, frequently asked questions, page or somewhere that they can get answers to their objections, whether it's via auto-responder or on the website itself.

✓ Be available for questions and feedback. A lot of on-line businesses these days are using something like humanclick.com that people can click on and talk with them immediately, or they go ahead and give their phone number and they do hold office hours. So you want to help people get their questions answered.

✓ Reply to their questions as quick as possible. We like to have a firm policy that we will answer emails within 48 hours, and we oftentimes answer them within hours. But we guarantee within 48 hours, excluding weekends. We will get back to them on Monday. It doesn't mean you have to reply to every single message you get, because you will get some that are absolutely irrelevant and they aren't even questions, or people just wanting to basically infringe on your time. So, you'll have to make those decisions on your own.

✓ Fill orders as quick as possible. If it's a digital product, you want your system set up so that it fulfills it immediately. If it's a shippable product, you'll want to get it out within 24 hours if possible.

© 2007 Shortcuts to Internet Millions, LLC - All Rights Reserved Worldwide
www.BigLeaguePlayersClub.com

✓ Ask for feedback. You need to get feedback from your customers. After they order, take them to a survey form and ask them a few more questions.

✓ Clear up problems promptly. If there's a problem on the site, you need to get it fixed. You can't let it linger. If there's something out of date, you have to get it fixed. You can't let it go on.

✓ You absolutely need to go out of your way to give excellent customer service. If you just do that, it will set you apart from the other companies because nobody is giving good customer service these days. They're ignoring people on-line.

And just doing these little things that we've mentioned above, will make you stand out and will bring your customers back to you over and over and over again.

Time Management

This is a list of things for you to do to organize your time and save time and money.

✓ Automation. Automate tasks that you have to do over and over again and are the same mundane things that take up time.

✓ Auto-responders. These are special email robots that send emails for you automatically around the clock.

✓ Use email filters in your email software to organize your emails.

✓ Use email reply templates (called stationary in Eudora) so you don't have to write responses from scratch and that will make answering questions easier and quicker.

✓ Use shortcut software. There are shortcuts available for download on the Internet that will memorize certain keystrokes so that you can just tell it one or two keystrokes and it will type out a whole string of information or it will perform tasks for you. So you can get this software to automatically fill out email addresses and signature files and web forms, and almost any other repetitive task.

✓ Real-time on-line credit card processing is another great time saver. So you don't have to manually process the orders that are coming in through the Internet.

✓ Have a FAQ list, frequently asked questions. This will save emails coming to you or phone calls coming to your office because people will be able to get their questions answered on-line.

✓ Set goals. If you don't know where you're going, you're not going to know how to get there. So you need to set the end result and set the goal for your Internet business and when you get off-track, adjust and try to get back on track.

✓ Use "To Do" lists. Take a lesson from all the top achievers; they're always using to do lists. As you add tasks to your to do list, be sure to write them in the order that you need to get them done, the highest priority first. Once your goals are set, you'll know which things on your to do list really need to get done, if you stay focused on the end result.

✓ Get a three-ring binder. You must get a three-ring binder to keep your project notes, your to do lists in, user name and passwords, phone numbers for your ISP, your hosting companies information, you'll need software and hardware specifications, you need all of this information at your fingertips.

© 2007 Shortcuts to Internet Millions, LLC - All Rights Reserved Worldwide

www.BigLeaguePlayersClub.com

✓ Don't forget about making the back-ups of your email lists and your hard drive or your important files.

✓ In an Internet business, virus software is an absolute must

✓ Set up a series of well thought out folders in your email program so that you can organize your emails, and filter it into those folders automatically. There is no need for all of your order emails that let you know someone ordered to come straight into your inbox. Those orders can be filtered and automatically filed in an "orders received" folder, that way email that you really need to tend to and reply to that's in your inbox, won't get missed because it's cluttered up by all kinds of other emails. People that automatically subscribe to your ezine, those should be filtered into a "subscription" box and that will keep your inbox clean and make it a lot easier to work with.

© 2007 Shortcuts to Internet Millions, LLC - All Rights Reserved Worldwide
www.BigLeaguePlayersClub.com

Chapter 6
Marketing Is Everything

That's what the saying says, anyway. In a nutshell, marketing is the process of informing prospects about your products and services, and then getting them to purchase those products and services. It really doesn't matter how great your product or service is if the world doesn't know about it and there will be no purchase. Someone once said, "Nothing happens until something is sold." Unfortunately, the marketing of most Internet businesses is very poor. There are a lot of products that are absolutely superior to the ones that are getting all the sales; it's just that people don't know about them because they're marketed incorrectly or very poorly. There are entire warehouses full of products that people can't sell even though they are superior to the ones that are really hot sellers on the market.

So, no matter what business you're in, you've got to be an effective marketer. You should actually consider yourself a marketer instead of the thing you're selling. In other words, you're not a plumber; you're a marketer of plumbing services. You don't sell an e-book on horseback riding; you're a marketer of horseback riding information products.

So, there are marketing strategies woven throughout these books that you have in your hands, but in this chapter we're going to focus on some specific ones. On the Internet, there are basically three models that we usually look at when we form an Internet business or start an Internet project.

1. A selling based model and this is where the real transaction is the sale of your own products and services, or you get commissions by promoting products and services of affiliate programs that you join
2. An advertising based model. In other words, you offer things to people, free things, discussion lists, or whatever, and it builds traffic or it builds a subscriber list. And then advertising on the site in the way of banner ads, text links, sponsor and classified ads in ezines generates the income
3. A combination of both 1 and 2, and this model actually combines a set of advertising on your website and in your ezines with the actual promotion and sale of products and services on your Internet site. And this is the actual model that we like to follow. The most successful model of marketing products and services that you own and control can be implemented very quickly and a subscriber base built up to also sell back-end products. So this is the best approach to take, but all three of them are available.

Give and Thou Shall Receive

The word "free" is looked for on the Internet. It's plain and simple. The Internet began as a mechanism to give free information away and so people often go to the Internet looking for stuff for free. So, there has been new ways devised of giving information away for free. And new ways are being innovated all the time. People are trying to figure out how to give something

© 2007 Shortcuts to Internet Millions, LLC - All Rights Reserved Worldwide

away for free so that the customer will be in a reciprocation position and feel obligated to also purchase something. So here are the types of free giveaways.

1.   Number one on the list is information. People usually put up a defense mechanism immediately to a sales pitch, just like when you walk into the car dealer, even though you're going there to buy a car, the sales people pounce on you and your defense mechanisms immediately go up. It's the same thing on the Internet. If people start sensing a pitch immediately, they get turned off. People generally don't like to be sold. So the alternative to that is to inform people and educate them, and in doing this you can give something away to them for free to read, a special report or an e-book. And then once they've had the time to kind of digest that information, then you can pull them in and market your way to a sale. So, information is a great thing to give away.

2.   Another thing that people give away is Internet services. I mean everyone that has an Internet business or is on the Internet needs Internet services. They give away web hosting for several months, they give away auto-responders, they give away email accounts and they give away chat rooms. That's how hotmail became such a huge product is they gave away free email accounts and then at the bottom of every email that went out, it said, "Hey, if you want your own free email account, just go to this place and sign up", and it became a huge seller.

3.   Software is another great free give away. The whole freeware and shareware industry is based on people giving away free software, and then once that free software is used, which is usually a reduced working version of the full fledged software package, if people like it and they want to get the full version, then they pay for that version. So, that's another great freebie.

Which Marketing Technique Is Best For Me

Well, except in very rare cases, the best strategy is to use a lot of strategies. We've seen Internet businesses that have become very successful on the back of one marketing strategy, it's possible but rare. However, if that one strategy ever stops, you may be in trouble. So you want to have multiple strategies in place. So we're going to talk about that right now. You'll see a little bit of overlap, but that's because of the synergistic values of these methods.

✓ **Individual emails.** You answer your prospect's questions via email and you want to gain a new customer by doing this. So, you can re-use previous emails to people over and over again to create new reply templates, and that was one of our time management methods. You also can use excerpts of previous emails. You can also use what's called a "signature file" in those emails and that's simply a tag line or brief classified ad after your name that goes at the bottom of your reply. So every time you reply to someone, there's a little bit of a promotion for your websites.

✓ **Articles.** You write articles, which you use as content in your own ezine. You can also post these articles on discussion boards and get them put on other web pages around the Internet, and they can draw traffic to your site. You can put them in particular forums or discussion lists and make them available. You can put a resource box, which is kind of like a signature file, after your name when you post in discussion forums letting people know that "if you want to get this free report or the rest of this information on this particular topic, go here". And then you can incorporate parts of the articles in your postings or you can put a number of articles into an e-book and provide it that way.

✓ **Your ezine or email newsletter.** You publish an ezine with solid information, information that helps and is of interest to your customer and prospect subscriber base and you use it to promote products and services. You sell sponsored and classified advertising like we mentioned. You use small ads and you can test new headlines. And so you want to also be cross-promoting other people's products in this newsletter.

✓ **Discussion boards**. You can put up your own discussion board. We have one of these at one of our sites and members end up talking to each other and helping each other out and it's a value-added service. And you can also go to public discussion boards and post answers to people's questions yourself and become somewhat of an expert on certain topics. You can trade links and banners on other people's discussion boards so that everyone that comes to the discussion board can see your banner and possibly click over to your site.

✓ **Your website itself**. You can use your website to build your subscriber list. You use your website to let buyers know about you and your company, its background, and simply giving away something free to generate email addresses. You use your website of course to make sales itself. You can use your website to earn commissions by promoting other people's products on your website. You can put articles on your website to attract people from other search engines because the search engines will come out and do what's called "spidering" and find your articles and if it's relevant it will post it on the search engine. You can also make your articles available to other people by posting them on your site and telling them they can use the article as long as they include your resource box. You can use your site to give away freebies, electronic books, your ezine, and of course the discussion board mentioned previously.

✓ **Information products.** You use your own information product to build your ezine subscriber list even though they may be purchasing a product. In that product you want to make sure you capture their email. You may have gotten this when they purchased, but you also, if you're giving away free information products, in those information products you want to make sure that they are clicking and subscribing to your ezine. You use these free information products also to make sales. You can put sales letters right inside the information products and it will bring people back to purchase from you.

So, as you can see, these things will all tie together and should overlap. You'll see many Internet marketers promoting all kinds of things and it just doesn't make sense, there doesn't seem to be any synergy there, and all the things that they are doing seem to be unrelated. So they never quite build that bond that they need with their customer base.

So whenever you are deciding on a new project, these are the things you should ask yourself:

a. Does this fit or reinforce the other things that I'm already doing or will it spread my time out too thin or will it dilute the other things I'm doing?
b. Does it fit in with what I'm already doing?

© 2007 Shortcuts to Internet Millions, LLC - All Rights Reserved Worldwide
www.BigLeaguePlayersClub.com

c. What parts of this project that I'm thinking about doing can be used in other areas of my business?

d. What parts of this particular opportunity can I repackage or recycle and use in other areas of my business?

Look at all the variety of products and services that you currently market and make sure that they're related to each other around a certain theme like horseback riding.

Diversifying is a good idea, but not just for the sake of diversifying and not at the risk of diversifying beyond your subject so much that it dilutes the power of the bond you have with that particular niche market.

How to Create a Profitable SIG File

This is a true secret. And I say this because I get so many emails that do not have signature files in them. So, it still has not caught on as widespread as it really should.

For those of you that don't know what a SIG file is, it's short for signature file and it's basically a little bit of text after your signature that might give a reader some information about you. It can be a straight advertisement, and you can use the signature file also when you post in news groups and any email or web-based discussion lists. But it's basically like a business card or a small classified advertisement. Its purpose is not to do a full sell job, but it's really to motivate them to click on some link or make some phone call or take some kind of action. And your signature file shouldn't be any longer than 60 characters long and maybe anywhere from 6 to 8 lines long; 3 to 6 lines is probably closer to what people expect. Here are some sample signature files:

```
--------------------------------------------------------------
Which marketing technique helped earn an average guy over
$25,000,000.00 (25 million) dollars starting with just a
$138 dollar ad, and enabled him to live the life of his
dreams? Do you know? Hint: Anyone can do what he did
-- use this technique and earn a fortune! Click here to learn
the answer: http://www.BigLeaguePlayersClub.com
--------------------------------------------------------------
Instant Profits: Which marketing technique helped earn an average
guy over $25,000,000.00 (25 million)dollars starting with just a
$138 dollar ad, and enabled him to live the life of his dreams?
http://www.BigLeaguePlayersClub.com
--------------------------------------------------------------
```

How to Create the Perfect Signature File

1. You want your signature file to really reach out and grab your prospect or your reader or your customer by the throat, and get them to look at it. You can use all caps, but you should only do this at the beginning of the signature file with maybe just the opening word so that it stands out and looks like a headline. You don't want to use all caps for the whole thing.

© 2007 Shortcuts to Internet Millions, LLC - All Rights Reserved Worldwide
www.BigLeaguePlayersClub.com

2. You want to target your signature file with the proper words. You might say, "Attention Horseback Riders", and then don't worry about catching the attention of people that aren't interested in your subject, because if you don't target then you are going to be wasting your efforts. It's better to reach 100 people that really want what you're talking about, then 10,000 people where none of them want what you're talking about.

3. Give away something free in your signature file. This can really boost your response and it should be something that has a high perceived value, but it doesn't cost you much. A free report or a free e-book oftentimes is a great freebie to give away.

4. You want to tell your prospects what's in it for them. In other words, whatever you might be asking them to do, you want to tell them why they should do it. You don't need to get involved in details of what they're going to get, but you need to give them one big benefit.

5. Whatever you want them to do or whatever you are asking them to do, make it easy for them to do it. Remember, they've got a lot of things on their mind and the easier you make things for them, the higher your response rate will be. So, you might give them an Internet address to go to. You might give them an auto-responder to send an email to. You might give them an email address to write to. You might give them a fax number to send something to, or a toll-free number.

6. Put a border around your signature file, like we've in our example and make it stand out from the rest of the message.

7. Avoid creating pictures out of your characters on your keyboard, in other words, don't use the letters O, L and K to build a nice little picture, because by the time it gets sent to people it will show up differently in their email program. Common practice is to create little logos out of the characters on the keyboard and type it into an email. The fact of the matter is it usually shows up all jumbled, so you really should avoid using what's called "ASCII art" in your SIG files.

8. The final item is test different versions of your SIG files. Send your ezine out one month with one SIG file, send it out another month with a different SIG file, or better yet, send out your ezine one month and send out half of it using one SIG file and the other half using a different SIG file. See if either of those SIG files draws more attention.

Use Many Different SIG Files

© 2007 Shortcuts to Internet Millions, LLC - All Rights Reserved Worldwide   www.BigLeaguePlayersClub.com
38

We have about six or seven different SIG files and we use them for different reasons. Here are some of the reasons that we have different SIG files:

If we're emailing someone that has responded to what was in our SIG file, then we use a different SIG file to let them know about something else we have.

We might mention our FAQ page or our ezine subscription or access to our order form to someone that has asked for that particular information.

If we're posted in news groups or email discussion groups, we sometimes will put a SIG file in it that will kind of match that particular news group.

If it's a colleague, then we sometimes will just put a SIG file that mentions all the websites that we have, but it doesn't really do much of a strong sell. So, you may create different SIG files for that reason. You always want to be doing something in your SIG file, but sometimes it may be more subtle than at other times.

© 2007 Shortcuts to Internet Millions, LLC - All Rights Reserved Worldwide

Chapter 7
How to Build A Stampede of Traffic to Your Website

Number one is, and we've mentioned it before and we're going to mention it again, do not use spam if you don't remember. In other words, you don't want to buy email lists of a million people and send out emails and bring them to your website. The fact of the matter is your website will be shut down very quickly. Opt-in email, where the user gives you permission to email them, on the other hand, can be very effective. We do have clients that simply buy opt-in lists, send emails to them, and those people come to their websites and purchase. But there are other even less expensive methods, and that is optimizing your website for search engines, building discussion boards, and giving away free e-books and other viral marketing tools.

So, we're going to focus on particular tools and give you a little bit of information on each one on how you can use them to build a stampede of traffic to your website.

Use Your Own Discussion Forum

Now, there are a lot of advantages to having discussion forums at your Internet site. Some of the advantages are:

They can generate a lot of traffic because what they'll do is people will come there and ask questions or they'll post information, and then other people will respond to that, and then people will enjoy being part of a group, it's human nature, and they like to be a part of a community. They will generate a lot of repeat traffic. People will post questions and oftentimes the feature of a discussion board is it sends you an email when someone replies to your questions. A discussion board can strengthen your credibility by building a brand name. And it can also demonstrate your expertise. If people are wanting to know about your subject and you truly know it inside out, they can be posting questions and as you're answering them, they will see you as an expert in their eyes and plus all the other visitors will see you as an expert also. It lets you demonstrate your expertise on a larger scale without having to take up hours and hours of phone conversations, for instance. A discussion board can generate leads and direct sales because you can promote, and if it's your own discussion board, you can have banner ads on it. You can also use your signature files and have links to areas of your website that actually sell products and services. Your discussion board can also generate advertising revenue. There is an opportunity to sell banner ads on your discussion board. So, here are some discussion forum traffic building ideas:

1. Start a thread of questions and answers yourself. In other words, post a question to motivate people to participate and ask them about something. And then they will start responding, and then you can respond back to that, and then you'll get a nice discussion going.
2. Ask your visitors what they want to see in the discussion forum and then do that for them.
3. Always be announcing your discussion forums in your ezine.

© 2007 Shortcuts to Internet Millions, LLC - All Rights Reserved Worldwide
www.BigLeaguePlayersClub.com

4. Post back issues of your ezine on your discussion board and then that will even add further content for people to read. And then you can invite your ezine readers to see those back issues, and then of course they will see the discussion board also.

5. Have guest moderators and have them come in and monitor a certain part of your discussion board and in exchange maybe you will let them put a banner on your discussion board or put a link to their product.

6. List your discussion forum in the right directories in search engines.

Final Points to Think About For Discussion Forums

A lot of places will offer to host your discussion forum for you. But all that does is bring traffic to their website. You should really host your discussion forum on your own website and then get the traffic advantages that we talked about.

You should moderate your own discussion board. You should also visit other discussion forums. However, this all can be very time consuming, so you want to maintain control over your time. You want to get other people to help moderate if you can. Many people will enjoy the process of being a moderator and helping out and being a little bit in the limelight. So if that makes sense for you, let them help.

There is a tendency of people to post advertising for their business and their products on your discussion forums without really contributing anything that's productive in the way of answering questions. And this really takes away the quality of a discussion board. The best ones are the ones that are moderated and people are told no advertising other than signature files.

Search Engine Traffic

While search engines and/or directories can be a big part of your web traffic, they're not as important as they used to be and the reason is because it's harder to master the search engines than it used to be, but it is one tool in the many ways that you're going to build traffic. And beside that fact, search engines are also always changing their criteria for getting listed. So, the advice we give you here might be different by the time you read the book. There is a lot of competition out there and there are a lot of sites and everybody's trying to get at the top of the search engines, so I suggest you follow the small advice here in this book, plus don't forget to read our companion search engine book.

How the Search Engines Rank Your Website

So how do the search engines actually decide who goes at the top of their results pages? Well, like we mentioned before, the criteria changes from time to time and it's actually different from one search engine to the next. The main consideration really is content. They are looking at your pages and it's reading the words on your pages for what are called "keyword phrases." And it's basically saying, "Hey, does this website really match up to this particular topic?" So here are a couple of elements from your web pages that actually have to do with keywords and they actually can affect your search engine ranking.

© 2007 Shortcuts to Internet Millions, LLC - All Rights Reserved Worldwide
www.BigLeaguePlayersClub.com

✓ The page title.
✓ The description meta tags.
✓ Keyword meta tags.
✓ How close to the top of the web page is your topic explained, i.e. if your topic is about marketing, do you have a headline very close to the top of the page that actually uses your keywords?
✓ The frequency of the keywords. In the old days, people used to put invisible words on their page and put the keywords over and over and over and over again, and this worked because the more time the keyword was listed, the more relevant the search engine thought your page was. Well, the search engines are smart enough not to fall for that anymore. However, they do look for the keywords to be sprinkled throughout your page at a certain rate, and these rates are always changing. There are software tools that can tell you the keyword relevancy and frequency on your pages.
✓ Finally, how close those keywords appear to each other. So again, if the keywords were right one after another and you listed them 100 times, the search engine would be on to that trick.

All the information about this topic is further explained in your Search Engine Magic Book and on your Internet Marketing Bible CD.

How to Get More Value from Your Site's Traffic

Getting a lot of website traffic is great. Taking advantage of it is even better. So, we're going to give you some tips now to utilize the traffic that's coming to your site. These tips will help you better analyze and take advantage of and strategize changes that need to be made.

So analyzing your traffic can reveal a lot of things about your visitors. Here are some of the things that you can find out:

❑ Which websites they were on before they came to your site.
❑ Which page they entered your site at.
❑ What type of browser they are using.
❑ The path they click through on your site.
❑ How much time they spent on your site.
❑ Which page they are on when they leave your site.
❑ Which pages are most popular and which ones are least visited.
❑ What errors are occurring while people are at your site.
❑ What search engines send you the most traffic?
❑ The exact number of visitors that a particular ad might send you.

Now, when you know information like this, you can adjust your site accordingly.

© 2007 Shortcuts to Internet Millions, LLC - All Rights Reserved Worldwide
www.BigLeaguePlayersClub.com

How to Analyze Your Internet Traffic

Here are some ways that you can actually analyze that traffic. One is use the statistic's program that your web host makes available to you and typically all you do is go out to the website analysis area and it gives you all the information that we just listed above.

Two is you could use special software that is made just for this purpose and it usually comes with a free version and a small paid fee version.

Hits vs. Visitors

Some often confuse hits with visitors. But they are not the same at all. Hits actually is a term that means every particular item on your page has been hit, in other words, your web page is a hit. If you have a banner on your web page, that's a hit. If you have any graphics showing pictures or maybe graphics of e-book covers, those are all hits. So you might have 10 or 12 items on a web page and that means it got 12 hits from just one visitor coming to it. However, visitors are actual single use visitors coming to your site. So they might go to different pages, but that's one visitor coming to your site. So you want to pay attention to unique visitors versus hits.

How to Handle "404 Errors"

This is a REAL secret. A 404 error is when somebody comes to your website and they either try to link to a page that's no longer there, or maybe they mistyped something and the page isn't available, and that's when you get those ugly "page cannot be found" errors.

When people come to your site and they get those, the tendency is to just move on. They just think that there's something wrong with the site, they may hit their back button and go back to the prior page and try something else, or they may just feel that the site that the page they were looking for is no longer available.

There is a unique little trick that you can do to handle what are called "http 404 file not found" errors. And the tip I'm going to give you is for what's called an "apache server", so there are other methods for other servers, but this is the most common. And what will happen is, if you follow the instructions I'm about to give you, when a user gets a 404 error, what will happen is instead of just getting a "page not found", you will take them to a custom page saying, "Hey, we realize that you tried to find something that maybe is not available on our site. It is either moved or possibly you mistyped something. If you'd like, you can get to these areas of our sites by clicking below." And then you can give them a menu of options to go to, or you can simply just transfer them to your home page. It's entirely up to you. But here's how to set up that default error page for an apache server.

There are four steps:

1. Open up your text editor and then create a new page and save it and call it ".htaccess". Okay, so now you have a new file.

© 2007 Shortcuts to Internet Millions, LLC - All Rights Reserved Worldwide
www.BigLeaguePlayersClub.com

2. Open up that .htaccess file and put the following two lines in that file. Line one is: "errordocument 404/error.htm". The next line is "errordocument 500/error.htm".

3. Now you want to create your custom error page that looks kind of like your other pages, but it gives them the ability to link to somewhere else on your site. You might say, "Sorry, but you tried to access a page that either has an error or it's not available anymore. But the links below will take you to other pages on our site."

4. You need to upload that file to what's called your home directory using ftp software. And you want to upload it in what's called "ASCII" mode.

Now test it by trying to go to a page that doesn't exist on your website, and once you get it working correctly, then you're going to get even more value out of your traffic that might have been lost by people getting page not founds.

© 2007 Shortcuts to Internet Millions, LLC - All Rights Reserved Worldwide

Chapter 8
How to Get Tons of Free Publicity

Most marketers are always trying to figure out how they're going to get more traffic and more sales and how much it's going to cost them. There are tons of free sources available. There are ways to get traffic for free, and we're going to give you some secrets that we've used to get tons of free publicity on the Internet and off the Internet. And you can get this free exposure also. It can be worth thousands and thousands, if not tens of thousands of dollars. I know from experience that these work. It's been a long time since we've only focused on paying for ads, however, we do pay for some ads and a lot of traffic we actually get for free. And this helps build our ezine subscriber base, it builds our sales, and it builds traffic to our affiliate programs that we promote also.

I'm sure that in a lot of businesses that are out there that just sell advertising, they would rather you not know about this because they are in the business of selling you stuff. But, that's too bad. We want you to keep as much money as you can of the income that you bring in on your Internet sales, and we don't want you blowing it on all the advertising. So we want you to get a lot of free advertising too, especially in the beginning when you maybe don't have the money to spend on some of the other paid advertising methods that we've given you, because the paid ads do have their place and times, but I recommend that you start with the free publicity strategies first.

With free publicity, you can get your name and your company and your products and services out to your markets on a regular basis and your goal can be to sell products and services, your goal can be to get leads for your ezine, your goal can be building traffic, your goal can be just developing credibility and getting your name out to your industry so they know you're available. Or your goal can be to make yourself an expert or authority on your particular subject.

Now many of these ways, even though they are billed as free advertising or free publicity may cost some amount of money, depending on the way you implement them. And they will cost time and effort, so there is a trade-off. However, the rewards far outweigh any investment of your resources that you will have to make and it is certainly better than going the paid advertising route only.

Paid Advertising vs. Free Publicity

An advantage of free publicity is that the audiences that see any information connected with you give it more credibility because you weren't paying for it. It's not a big paid advertisement. So, if other people are writing about you and they happen to think that source is credible such as a newspaper or a particular ezine or website, that credibility translates over to you because they have mentioned you. However, if you pay to run an ad that doesn't give you as much credibility.

© 2007 Shortcuts to Internet Millions, LLC - All Rights Reserved Worldwide

Free publicity is much harder to get than paid advertising sometimes though, because if you pay for advertising you can pretty much bet that your ad is going to be put in. However, free publicity, they get information about people all the time and only certain pieces of information actually get publicized. So, despite that, free publicity is still worth going after and there are a lot of techniques that can improve your chances of getting free publicity.

Using Articles to Get Free Publicity

Now this free publicity strategy really ties into what we've talked about before as far as getting subscribers to your ezine. Editors are always looking for material for their publications. We've gotten countless articles printed in trade magazines and ezines. Editors don't always have the time to prepare all of this content themselves or their writers don't always have the time, so they're always looking for outside sources. And if you provide them with great content, they will publish you regularly. So that's where we come in for the free publicity. We provide them with great articles and sometimes they archive these articles and you can end up with long-term links from their site back to yours. In 1998 Jim wrote an article one site posted and it still sends traffic over from their trade association site that has archived their articles. We still get visitors and make sales. So, there are only a couple of steps to get great free publicity using articles:

1. Of course, match those topics to the interests that your target market has.
2. Create informative articles based on whatever the hot topic is.
3. Build your list of media sources.
4. Submit your articles to those sources.
5. Keep expanding your media list all the time and keep using it over and over again and you'll steadily reach a larger and larger potential readership through your articles.

So, let's go through each of these steps one by one.

1. Determine the Topic of Your Target Market

That's what we've really been teaching you about marketing. We need to find out what they want, what their needs are, and then we want to push those hot buttons. What interests do they have, and if you know the field well, you probably know these things already. And if you've got your finger on the pulse of your market, it shouldn't be very hard for you to come up with these topics. So, you simply write articles that show readers how to get something that they want, or how to avoid something they want to stay away from. It's the old pleasure and pain principle.

You want to remember this very important point, which applies to all your marketing or business activities, the focus should not be on you.

If, in your article you are always talking about you, that's not going to be of any benefit to your readers. Your focus has to be on helping the readers and the subscriber base or the customers to get what they want or stay away from what they don't want. It's got to help them achieve some type of pleasure or help them avoid some type of pain. And if you deliver these benefits in your articles, then you're going to be converting prospects to first time customers, and you will also be retaining loyal customers and nudging them to buy more and more.

© 2007 Shortcuts to Internet Millions, LLC - All Rights Reserved Worldwide
www.BigLeaguePlayersClub.com

2. Creating Articles Based On What Your Market Wants

It's best to really cultivate the skill of writing your own articles. If you haven't mastered it, it would be very beneficial to you if you do. Even if you're not a great writer, it's something you can develop. All you have to do is find articles that you like and rewrite them with a pencil and paper, and continue to do this, and over a period of time you'll be able to write your own articles. So, in addition to writing articles, you're going to be writing to prospects, you're going to be sending out emails, posting to news groups, so this little exercise will help you in all of your writing. And even the best writers make tons of mistakes, but readers tend to be picky, so while the lack of good writing skills may not reflect how you run your business, it might distract from the points that you're trying to make. So, you want to have a good spell checker, you want to have somebody read your articles, you may read them yourself out loud to see how they sound, and if you really are a poor writer, then you really want to hire someone because this is a great technique for free publicity. So, whichever way you go, whether you're writing your own or whether you're hiring someone, you want to make sure you get full copyright ownership of these articles.

And here are some elements of a good revenue or profit building article.

Your article needs to get the attention of the prospects.

You need to have a great headline that snares them in. You need to demonstrate your knowledge of the problems that they are facing, in other words, how are you going to help them achieve what they want or avoid the pain that they want to be relieved of.

You need to demonstrate your expertise and how you can help them.

The article needs to build your credibility

It needs to gain your prospect's trust or your reader's trust.

It then of course, needs to motivate your readers to take action.

The Importance of a Headline

I want to step back and talk about the headline. You've probably heard this. We've mentioned this in our other materials, but think about how you read the newspaper. It's based on looking at headlines. You see a headline that catches your attention, you then read the article. It's the same with your articles. You need to have a great headline, something that will draw people in. And it really shouldn't be cute or a cliché or a joke. You need to have a big benefit oriented headline that tells them in essence what they're going to get out of reading this article. So, you want to be laser focused and you want to write out 20, 30, 40 or 50 different headlines as we do when we write our headlines. And once your headline does the job and gets their attention, then they'll start reading. And then after that, you need to make sure that every single word and every single paragraph in your article leads them to read the next one.

© 2007 Shortcuts to Internet Millions, LLC - All Rights Reserved Worldwide

Now, in return for publishing your articles, most of your media outlets will include the resource box at the end of the article. In fact, we just refuse to even let them use an article unless they include our resource box. Some of them will even let you put more of an ad at the bottom but, at the minimum, you should have a resource box that may do a number of things:

(a) It might get them to buy your products immediately
(b) It might ask them to get more information from you, which is of course moving them along the path to buying
(c) It might ask them to take action and let them know that you're going to follow-up. In other words, it might have them subscribe, it might have them send to an auto-responder or request some type of free report. And it's best to give them multiple options like we mentioned before.

We've listed a typical resource box below.

```
------------------------------------------------------------------
Which marketing technique helped earn an average guy over
$25,000,000.00 (25 million) dollars starting with just a
$138 dollar ad, and enabled him to live the life of his
dreams? Do you know? Hint: Anyone can do what he did
-- use this technique and earn a fortune! Click here to learn
the answer: http://www.BigLeaguePlayersClub.com/
------------------------------------------------------------------
```

And since your resource boxes are very much like signature files, you should go back and reread the section on signature files as well. And if they give you a choice between a free ad or a resource box, I would take the free resource box because it's going to go right after your article, and people are going to be reading the article and then they'll have a chance to act on the resource box. Whereas, we don't know what will happen if we just run an ad. If they'll do more than one article, then maybe you try both ways, but we recommend you get full benefit out of your article and that is using a resource box right after it.

3. Building Your List of Media Sources

Now building a good list of media sources can be an absolute goldmine. And continuing to expand this and develop relationships with media contacts can be very profitable. You go through different print and on-line publications that have to do with your particular market, you'll find mention of other publications that also might have opportunities for you to run articles in. So, you can slowly build up a nice media list. It's not uncommon for us to subscribe to ezines that have to do with our target market that we're working on and I might not have any interest in reading them, but I'll look through them for other opportunities that they mention. So, you want to look for requests for article submissions, you want to look for mentions of other publications, and any other kind of information that will turn you on to additional free publicity avenues.

4. Sending Your Articles to Your Media Outlets

© 2007 Shortcuts to Internet Millions, LLC - All Rights Reserved Worldwide

You need to find out how your media outlets want your articles. Some want them fast so they'll want them emailed. Some will want them in a word processing format. Some will want them in a text format. So, you actually keep this list of media sources in a document and then go to each source and then find out how they want your articles sent, and then you need to prepare them that way and send them to each outlet in the format that they want them. Otherwise, they will just trash them. Some may want them mailed to them on computer diskettes. So, you really need to make sure they get them in the proper format.

It's very smart to handle your media outlets just the way you would a subscriber list. In other words, put together an email list and then email merge a notification of new articles available and you can use some of the software programs that we've mentioned. But what you do is you want to let them know that you have articles available and maybe there is a new article and you can send out an email and you can personalize it and tell them what's available. Now, you always want to give them the ability to get off your article notification list. Very few will because they are looking for articles. And then you want to make it very easy for them to get your article from you, so it's either make a phone call, send an email, a fax, go to an auto-responder and the article will come back to them. So you want to make it very easy.

5. Expanding Your Media Resource List

Now, we've developed our initial list, we've got it customized, we started submitting articles to it, we're getting free publicity. This is not where we want to stop. We want to create a snowball effect. We want to get more and more free publicity, so you've got to do two things; continue expanding that list, and then make previous articles available. And as you are continuing to expand your list by the ways we've already talked to you about, plus by being alert all the time to always record new media possibilities, and the only way to really do this is to set aside time to work on it. And then every time you submit articles to your media list, and you should be doing this at least once a month, you want to make sure to include information on how they can get previous articles. And then by offering a variety of articles to select from, there might be a better chance that the publisher will select at least one of those articles, and maybe they'll even run multiple articles. And then as your media list expands, you'll be in a position to reach more and more prospects through your articles.

One final thought on using articles for free publicity. One of the easiest ways to make them available for other publishers is to put them on your website and let them download them for free. We've seen articles generate thousands and thousands of dollars worth of free publicity, and you can do this too. In fact, we'd be glad to know when you've gotten your first $1,000 worth of free publicity. Just send us a note letting us know.

Getting Free Publicity Using Press Releases

Now press releases are another great tool to use and they can bring in a lot of web traffic. They can bring in subscribers, leads, sales and everything else that goes with it. In comparison to the benefits that go with it, the small investment can be very worth it and for the best

© 2007 Shortcuts to Internet Millions, LLC - All Rights Reserved Worldwide
www.BigLeaguePlayersClub.com

effectiveness, a press release needs to be newsworthy and it needs to be informative to the audience. It needs to be written properly, and it needs to be targeted to the right media outlets.

How to Create Your Press Release to Be Newsworthy

Editors are always looking for news and they're looking for information that will be of interest to their audience, and a good press release will make their job a lot easier. Your press release automatically will be thrown out if it's just a self-serving pitch for a product. The goal is to make it appear newsworthy and informative.

How to Write Your Press Release

You always want to begin with the words "New Release" or "For Immediate Release" at the top of your company letterhead. Also at the top, include the contact information like your name, company, address, phone, fax, email address, and website. And below that contact info, you want to have a descriptive headline, just like any other headline, it needs to grab their attention. And then the body copy of your press release needs to hold their attention. You want to start the news release off with a very strong benefit that's really targeted and focused on your prospects or the readers. Then you want to follow that up with, of course, another benefit and on and on. This is where the market research comes in. It will tell you what benefits the audience really wants. And another thing about your press release is that it should start with the most important benefit because if any information has to be cut out, the editors will usually start at the bottom of the press release.

How Do You Make Your Press Release Newsworthy?

Well, what's unique or unusual about your offer? What's going on in the world today that maybe you can link it to? Is there a holiday or is there a current event? How can you make it informative and worthwhile to read? When you're writing your press release, you need to ask questions just like a good reporter would. Who, what, when, where, why and how? And then you need to answer them. You need to put the emphasis on the benefits that your products and services are going to give to the readers and you want to show how it helps them gain something or avoid something like we talked about earlier. Solving a problem or achieving a goal. Offer something for free, if possible, especially something that has a high perceived value, but it won't cost you very much. Now a free report on-line or e-book is a natural, low cost thing you can offer for free and it quite often will garner you an email address. You want to make your press release look professional.

Now you want to have complete follow-up information included on all your press releases so prospects will know how to contact you or how to get the free information. That's the whole purpose behind writing a press release to begin with. And it's best to limit this whole press release to what would be one printed page or, in the case of an email, to maybe one full screen one.

Target the Right Media Outlets

© 2007 Shortcuts to Internet Millions, LLC - All Rights Reserved Worldwide
www.BigLeaguePlayersClub.com

Now once you have this press release, you need to send it to the right places. And if it's not relevant to the interest of a certain audience, there's no reason for that media outlet to get it. And if they continue to get press releases from you that don't pertain to their audience then when you have one that will pertain to their audience they will more than likely still be throwing them out. And even if they do run it, you'll be reaching the wrong people. So send your news release to the right media outlets, and if you have the person's name, try to make it attention to a specific individual. And the more media outlets you can send your release to, as long as they are your target market, the greater chance will be of getting media attention and free publicity. And you also want to give priority to media, which is closest, absolutely most targeted to your market and then go to the less promising ones after that. There are also press release submission services that will submit your press release to all the media outlets and we recommend these services.

© 2007 Shortcuts to Internet Millions, LLC - All Rights Reserved Worldwide

Chapter 9
How to Create Web Sites That Sell!

Millions of dollars in sales has revealed the basic ingredients of what makes a web site successful as a direct response marketing tool.

A direct response marketing tool is where someone is directed to take an action. It could be to pick up a phone and call, e-mail for more info, or fill out an order form and order online or sign up for something.

Unless your website's just a business card site to get your name "out there" or it's an Entertainment or Informational site you really have a "direct response" site. You want the visitor to do something right?

How do we tilt the tables in our favor so that visitors to our site will respond in the way we want them to?

Well, here is what is happening with current web pages that are doing very well as direct response tools:

1. The site must load fast and the faster the better.
2. The benefit to the customer must be clear, compelling, and stated early in the message.
3. Choices should be limited. Taking action one way or another and all actions should lead to closing the sale or getting the required response.
4. The offer should be risk free and trustworthy.

#1 – The site must load fast

Remember in the old days you expected it. Click on something and then take a break while it loaded. Not anymore. With cable modems, DSL and more people online, more options and other places to go; people don't want to wait any longer.

It's critical that your visitor not wait to receive your message. If they have to wait:

✓ They become impatient and "click away" to another site.
✓ If they stay around to "wait", they get frustrated and they are already negative toward your site. This makes the sell job that much harder.

I'll assume at this point you believe fast loading pages are a must and get right to how to accomplish this.

© 2007 Shortcuts to Internet Millions, LLC - All Rights Reserved Worldwide
www.BigLeaguePlayersClub.com

Logos, Images, Backgrounds, and Icons

These usually are the things that slow down page loading.

Logos – Your site should be professional but it doesn't require a big fat log graphic. Most people don't care about your logo as much as YOU do. They want to know "what benefit you have to offer them" and how can you help them "solve their problem". You should keep your logo if you are going to use one to about one-third of the top of the page. Either centered or off to the left with a compelling headline along side, or directly under. You should always have a caption with a picture; this is an old direct response principle. The file byte size of the Logo should be no larger than 6K, and smaller is better.

Backgrounds - Plain backgrounds work best. White or off-white are still the most popular. Backgrounds with a left hand margin present a professional image with the added benefit of making the text easier to read -- since the lines are shorter and more resemble a magazine's familiar format. Background Images can be used but they should be no larger than 3K.

Images - Only used if they are essential to the offer. A product picture could be classified as essential depending on the product. If you are selling a car, the visitor will want to see a picture of the car and the picture's purpose is to make the site visitor contact you. It is obvious that they probably won't buy the car from your site so the action is to start a dialogue by contacting you. The "direct response" you are looking for in this case is e-mail or phone call. All of your images should be geared to motivate your site visitor to take one of those two very specific actions.

Here are some file "byte size" guidelines from our programmer.

Under 10K - best
10K - 20K - acceptable if the picture is really important
20K - 30K - the picture better be damn important
Over 30K - find a way to make it smaller or put a thumbnail and link to bigger picture.

Icons - These should be tiny, whenever possible under 1K; and seldom larger than 3K.

By the way, you can find tons of INTERNET graphics professionals. Test them by having them create great graphics that enhance the image and load fast.

When possible re-use the same background, logo, icons, and images throughout your site. The way a computer works is that it stores the images on the visitor's computer while he's looking at the web page. That means as they move through your site, the next web page that uses a previously viewed graphic will load faster because the graphic will already be saved to their computer for viewing.

© 2007 Shortcuts to Internet Millions, LLC - All Rights Reserved Worldwide
www.BigLeaguePlayersClub.com

Another guideline from our programmer - The overall byte size of your page, with text and all other components should be no larger than 20K - 30K. These are only guidelines to shoot for.

Obviously, some "picture dependent" sites cannot be designed within these guidelines. Just make sure every picture is essential to your offer and you have made every effort to optimize the page's loading speed.

Just always be asking yourself…. "do I really need this graphic?"

#1 - The benefit to the customer must be clear, compelling, and stated early in the message.

If the customer does not find a benefit early in your page, they will usually click away, there is too much to see on the Internet.

Ideally, the biggest benefit should be in a headline at the top of the page and should NOT have to compete with a logo. The customer wants to know, "what's in it for me" right away!

Like so many other poorly designed websites, if you choose your company's mission statement as a headline you will lose most visitors.

#2 - Choices should be limited. Taking action one way or another and all actions should lead to closing the sale or getting the required response.

Most web pages offer too many choices. Because of the nature of "hypertext" linking, web designers feel compelled to give visitors a lot of opportunities to "click away" before the product or service message has been fully delivered. This is one of the most common mistakes being made on the Internet today. Everything is competing with your message for the visitor's attention.

You should carefully consider where your links are sending your visitors. If you are looking for your visitor to take action on your offer, then you should only include choices that will move them closer to that decision.

Offer too many choices and people give up. In fact, most people are begging to be led so help them out, tell them what to do. The hardest objection in the world to overcome is "I'll think about it" so don't let them use that one. Don't give them time to think about it, keep them moving and show them the way.

#3 The offer should be risk free and trustworthy.

Be prepared to offer certain guarantees that your product will do what you say. Today's consumer is very jaded after being ripped off so many times with inferior products. The strategy by some is called risk reversal. It's your product, shouldn't YOU take the risk? Rather than the customer?

© 2007 Shortcuts to Internet Millions, LLC - All Rights Reserved Worldwide

I already know your first thought; won't everybody return things for a refund?

Yes some will - those that don't like the product or don't think it does what it says it does and of course those deadbeats that like to take advantage when they can.

However, the increase in "refunds" will be dwarfed by the extra business you do because of the great guarantee you were giving. As long as you have a quality product that is, that does what it says it will do, people will keep it.

© 2007 Shortcuts to Internet Millions, LLC - All Rights Reserved Worldwide
www.BigLeaguePlayersClub.com

Chapter 10
The Final Word

We want to thank you for reading this book and staying with us. We've tried to share effective strategies and ideas and tools that we've used and our associates have used and our clients have profited from about how to market on-line and things to consider to make your Internet business a success.

Just as we have left the boredom and grind of the corporate world and working for someone else to make a living here at home with mail order and Internet marketing, it's my desire that you will go through all of these books and do the same thing, if that is your goal. We certainly have tried to give you the advantage over not having any of this information when starting your Internet business. These are all resources that we didn't have when we started out and that we gained as we went along the way. You'll find other resources as you continue along this path of freedom from the rat race.

Now keep in mind that a lot of the marketing principles that we've listed in this book are actually timeless. They have been true for mail order before the Internet was available, and they've been true on the Internet since it's been available.

Here's to your future success!

Jeff

Remember for the latest updates and latest news register for your "Free Gift" at
http://www.BigLeaguePlayersClub.com

© 2007 Shortcuts to Internet Millions, LLC - All Rights Reserved Worldwide